31 Days Toward Trusting God's Promises

Puddles and Rubber Boots

A Devotional Book

Jeanie M. Fritz

Photography, cover design, and book layout: Michael Fritz, Fritz Photography

Printed in the United States of America.

ISBN-13:978-1978256972
ISBN-10: 1978256973

To my husband and best friend, Michael,
and to our precious son, Isaiah Daniel,
and in memory of our baby, Aaron David.

Contents

Puddles and Rubber Boots

I have always liked wearing rubber boots. As I child, I fondly remember running in wet spring fields, playing in mud puddles, and exploring woodland groves—all while wearing my trusty rubber boots. Some people find rubber boots to be clumsy, squeaky, and unattractive. However, I am not above having a pair of rubber boots in my wardrobe. I currently trollop around in a cherry red pair with buckles. Rubber boots keep me dry, warm, and happy.

Just as rubber boots help me to face a rainy day with cheerful courage, God's Word gives me the emotional strength to face every spiritual storm. We all encounter storms in our lives; we can't control them. Sometimes these personal problems last for years, even decades; other times, we endure a particularly intense season of pain, followed by a dull ache. However, we can choose to face the rain, puddles, and mud of life with joy, hope, and faith. God's assurances of salvation and help are true. The promises of His Word never fail, and they are extended to every believer.

When facing suffering, I have often wished for a devotional book that would explore the promises of God's Word. My personal quest to find and understand Divine truth has inspired me to write the meditations found in this book.

In the spring of 2017, when my baby boy was stillborn, God told me in prayer to testify to others of His goodness and to praise Him for His faithfulness. I promised God I would. Right now, my hands could be cradling a newborn, feeding and caring for my son. Instead, in obedience to God, I have thrown my energies into writing these meditations—my affirmation of faith in my Sovereign, Loving Lord.

Reflections

Each meditation ends with reflection questions, which I hope will inspire you in your walk with God. If a question does not resonate with you, consider writing about the promise Scripture or suggested Scripture passage. Finally, *Puddles and Rubber Boots* can be used in small group Bible studies with the reflection prompts serving as a springboard for public discussion.

Where the Rubber Meets the Road

At the end of each meditation, I have synthesized a key truth into one line. These truths in my opinion are where the rubber meets the road. I hope you gain comfort from these truth tidbits, and they are a like a pair of rubber boots for you, keeping you warm and dry as you face the storms of your day.

I hope this devotional book will reassure you during the storms of your life—the voice of a friend speaking to you through the wind and the darkness. I want to remind all my readers God's promises are sure, and He never fails. May you feel God's embrace. I pray God will draw you closer to Himself, making you more like Him.

In Christian love,
Jeanie Fritz

Part One

When I Struggle to Trust God

For my thoughts are not your thoughts, neither are your ways my ways, saith the Lord.

Isaiah 55:8 (KJV)

Day 1

Healed with Spit

Scripture Reading: Mark 8:22-26

Promise from God: For my thoughts are not your thoughts, neither are your ways my ways, saith the Lord. For as the heavens are higher than the earth, so are my ways higher than your ways, and my thoughts than your thoughts.

Isaiah 55:8-9 (KJV)

In reading the eighth chapter of Mark, have you ever wondered why Jesus spit on the blind man to heal him? After all, Jesus, all powerful and one with God, helped create the world according to John 1. God spoke every part of creation into being with just words. Jesus also healed with verbal commands and sometimes a gentle touch. However, Mark tells us on two different occasions Jesus spit on people as He healed them.

In Mark chapter 8, Jesus healed a man with blindness after first spitting on his eyes. According to the wisdom of the day, saliva had healing properties and was considered an appropriate treatment for blindness. However, the man in Mark 8 was looking for a miracle. After hearing Jesus speak healing to others, I'm sure this man with blindness was expecting an instant and complete healing.

I wonder if this poor man was surprised by Jesus' methods. After Jesus partially restored his sight, the man with blindness could have stumbled away saying, "I don't understand. Why did He spit on me? What is going to happen now? I can't even see anything clearly—just shapes and colors. I'm disappointed in this Healer. I trusted Him. I thought He was God, but He doesn't seem to have much power after all."

This story of Jesus' gradual healing with spit illustrates for me that sometimes God's will does not seem elegant, sensible, or understandable. When we expect God to move instantly and completely, we are often disappointed. Amid a storm or trial, we wring our hands; we complain. "How can God be at work in this situation?" we mourn. "Nothing about this circumstance makes any sense." Maybe we can see the beginnings of a miracle; but all the pieces have not fallen into place, so we begin to doubt. And besides, we are uncomfortable. We may feel physically and emotionally miserable, like the poor man with spit running down his face. Surely, God has it all wrong. We expected instant victory or deliverance—not redemption in stages, and we certainly didn't expect such an assault upon our self-respect in the process. It feels as if God is spitting on us.

In Isaiah 55:8, God tells us, "For my thoughts are not your thoughts, neither are your ways my ways." While we have a picture in our heads of how God should work, His plan is often far greater than we could ever have imagined. So, next time when the spit is running down our faces, let's remember to pause and tell Jesus, "I'm not sure why you have asked me to suffer, but I'm going to trust you anyway. I leave the outcome to you."

Reflection

Have you ever prayed over a troubling situation with discouraging results? How was the hand of God at work, even though everything looked hopeless?

_____

_____

_____

_____

How will you feel if God does not answer one of your current prayers in the way you expect?

_____

_____

_____

_____

Complete this thought: I will continue to trust God even when "His ways are not my ways" because _____

_____

_____

_____

 Where the Rubber Meets the Road

Expect God to work in unexpected ways; He specializes in surprises.

Day 2

An Easter Epiphany

Scripture Reading: John 12:20-32

Promise from God: Verily, verily, I say unto you, Except a corn of wheat fall into the ground and die, it abideth alone: but if it die, it bringeth forth much fruit. He that loveth his life shall lose it; and he that hateth his life in this world shall keep it unto life eternal.

John 12:24-25 (KJV)

Little did I know 2012 would be a watershed year for my husband and me. Easter season rolled around. Outside, tulips and daffodils were blooming in red and yellow waves; forsythia bushes were ablaze like sunshine across our lawn. Inside, my mind and heart were a roiling mess. A public-school teacher, I was about to be laid off due to budget cuts. My job was our family's main source of income while my husband worked through another college degree. We had purchased our first home; I had student loans, and the cost of living was high. Without my job, we faced losing all the financial ground we had gained as a young couple.

However, in emotional and spiritual terms, life had never been better. Several years of personal counseling and participation in a small group at a local church had brought me to this realization: God was calling me to a deeper walk with Him. Was I willing to follow? God was asking me in the place of prayer to reject the American Dream and devote my life to full-time Christian service. Could I die out to my own goals, ambitions, and desires? Could I surrender everything to God?

By Easter Sunday, the answer was, "Yes, I can, and I will." I like to call it my Easter Epiphany. "Take my career, my job, my house, my finances, my dreams, my marriage, and myself," I told God. And He did just that. Two months later I was laid off from my job. My husband, who had a call to ministry, had also re-consecrated his life to God. Four months later, we were packing up and moving across the state to enter full-time ministry.

In three-years' time, God blessed us with a baby boy, and I became a stay-at-home mom and homemaker. Even then, God required me to keep dying out to my own dreams and desires. I pictured a home full of children; but after several years and three pregnancies, I had only one child on this earth. God chose to take two of my babies to Heaven. But still I know that surrendering my entire self to Christ was the right choice. God has a Divine purpose for the troubles I have faced, and I continue to trust Him. Though dead to self, I've never been more alive.

The secret to life is death—death to selfishness, to self-ambition, to our own understanding, and death to anything and everything that God says must be eradicated. Speaking of his own death and resurrection, Jesus said, "Verily, verily, I say unto you, Except a corn of wheat fall into the ground and die, it abideth alone: but if it die, it bringeth forth much fruit. He that loveth his life shall lose it; and he that hateth his life in this world shall keep it unto life eternal" (John 12:24-25). Jesus died that we might have life. He also was the example of consecration that every Christian must follow if he or she will attain eternal life.

Paul said in Galatians 3:20, "I am crucified with Christ: nevertheless I live; yet not I, but Christ liveth in me: and the life which I now live in the flesh I live by the faith of the Son of God, who loved me, and gave himself for me." We must be crucified with Christ that we might truly live.

Suffering, surrender, and crucifixion are the only means that we "may know him, and the power of his resurrection." As Jesus Himself said, "He that loveth his life shall lose it; and he that hateth his life in this world shall keep it unto life eternal" (John 12:25).

Reflection

How have you experienced crucifixion and resurrection in your spiritual life?

_____

_____

_____

_____

What do you need to surrender to God today?

_____

_____

_____

_____

How has God promised to bring fruit from our suffering if we will die out to self?

_____

_____

_____

_____

 Where the Rubber Meets the Road

Death to self leads to abundant life in Christ.

Day 3

Trust the Captain

Scripture Reading: Mark 4:35-41

Promise from God: And he arose, and rebuked the wind, and said unto the sea, Peace, be still. And the wind ceased, and there was a great calm.

Mark 4:39 (KJV)

The waves were breaking over their heads. The boat was already filling with water. Soaked to the skin, their muscles tiring with the struggle, they had weathered many storms; yet even the veteran fishermen were afraid. This storm was a monster; they didn't see how they could survive.

As the Son of God, Jesus knew this storm was coming; yet he had asked them, the disciples, to launch out in the boat—to cross the Sea of Galilee. It didn't make sense. When the disciples called out to Jesus in the storm, maybe they were confused as well as afraid. Had they not obeyed Jesus by sailing out into the sea? Why then were they facing a deadly storm?

And through it all, Jesus was in the back of the boat—sleeping. The storm raged on, but He was quiet. They received no comforting words or promises of strength—just deathly silence from their Leader, their Captain.

We, like the disciples, often face storms where God seems silent. Satan creeps up to us, and He whispers in our ear, "God knew this was going to happen, and He didn't even warn you. He could have stopped this. If He loves you, He should end your suffering." And the storm we face threatens to destroy us—eroding our faith, our peace, and our hope.

Satan also tempted the disciples to doubt because they woke Jesus up with the words, "Don't you care that we are going to die?" There wasn't much faith in their question, and Jesus rebuked them for it.

Jesus was disappointed that after all the miracles they had witnessed, they did not trust Him to protect them from the storm.

We, like the disciples, also sometimes struggle to trust God in fierce winds and waves. In our minds, we know God is sovereign. He could stop the storm at any time. Why doesn't He? And we call on God—plead with Him—finding acceptance only when we hear Him say, "Peace, be still." Sometimes He calms the storm; it abates. Other times it rages on; but God calms us, assuring us that He is still there. He is in the boat with us; it will not sink. God is bigger than the storm. He knows that the storm is not going to destroy us, if we will trust in Him.

Reflection

When have you obeyed God and then faced a difficult storm as a result?

_____

_____

_____

_____

Why is it difficult to trust God when we have tried to do His will and then face problems?

_____

_____

_____

_____

How can you find peace, knowing that God is bigger than the storm?

_____

_____

_____

_____

 Where the Rubber Meets the Road

Trust the captain of the ship.

Part Two

When I Lack Strength

This is my comfort in my affliction: for thy word hath quickened me.

Psalm 119:50 (KJV)

Day 4

Clinging to
God's Words

Scripture Reading: Psalm 119:41-56

Promise from God: This is my comfort in my affliction: for thy word hath quickened me.

Psalm 119:50 (KJV)

M any people experience depression during the turbulence of adolescence. It happened to me. I developed severe depression and generalized anxiety at age 11. I was 15 before I came out of the long, dark tunnel.

Nights were the worst. I would lay awake, my mind torturing me with fear and despair. My parents were always there for me. Unable to sleep and feeling emotionally low, I would often go to my parents' bedroom door and call out to them in the middle of the night. Either my dad or mom would get up and talk with me. We would go to the living room and sit on the couch, and my parents would listen as I poured out my heart—all the things I could not say during the daylight hours. Their human words and assurances provided some comfort.

On my thirteenth birthday, my aunt gave me a special promise Bible published by Christian Heritage Publishing house. Over 2,000 promises of God were highlighted in the text. "As you read them, consider them personal, and know God will never break His promises to His people," the editors admonished in the Bible's introduction.

Some nights instead of waking my parents, I would get out my promise Bible and read the Psalms, carefully dwelling on all those highlighted verses in their context. Sometimes I would underline in black ink the promises that really resonated with me. Those squiggly, shaky underlines represented my life—unsteady, uncertain, but clinging to God's words as my only hope.

Over the years, I have gained so much comfort from reading the promises of God's Word—learning about His holy, but merciful and loving nature—and seeing God work His promises out within my life. Depression and its twin, anxiety, have haunted me at various points in my life. For many years, I can be several steps ahead of them; but during times of difficult change or loss, they catch up with me, dogging my steps. I still cling to the promises of God during those dark times, especially the assurances of the Psalms.

I use a different Bible now. However, the other morning, I pulled out the Bible I had so savored as a teenager. I looked at some of the promises I had underlined. How precious God's promises still were to me, but how far I had come! God had increased my faith over the past three decades. I no longer struggled to believe God's promises were for me. I believed them whole-heartedly—they were the words of my Father. His Word had been my comfort through affliction. God Himself had been more faithful to me than I could ever have imagined, and sometimes God had seemed closer to me than most people. I had learned to talk to Him about everything. His words from Scripture were deep within my heart. I had found God's Word not only gives comfort during a time of crisis, but His eternal and immutable commands and promises provide long-term strength—my only strength. As the Psalmist said, "This is my comfort in my affliction: for thy word hath quickened me" (Psalm 119:50).

Reflection

How have you found God's Word to be a source of comfort and strength in the past?

_____

_____

_____

_____

What can we gain from reading, studying, and meditating on God's Word?

_____

_____

_____

_____

How can you spend more time dwelling on Scripture? List three specific changes you can implement in your life to make Scripture a greater part of your day.

_____

_____

_____

_____

 Where the Rubber Meets the Road

If we dwell in God's Word, it will become our life-long refuge.

A Blooming Rosebud

Scripture Reading: 2 Corinthians 12:7-10

Promise from God: And he said unto me, My grace is sufficient for thee: for my strength is made perfect in weakness. Most gladly therefore will I rather glory in my infirmities, that the power of Christ may rest upon me.

2 Corinthians 12:9 (KJV)

A friend of our family sent us a bouquet of old-fashioned roses cut from her garden. My niece brought the roses home carefully wrapped in wet paper towels. I immediately plunged the long green stems into a vase of water. The flowers had beautiful, silken petals—in vivid reds, pinks, whites, mauves, and fuchsias—no two roses were alike. I was disappointed when I woke up the next morning and saw one of the rosebuds had wilted. This flower bud won't survive, I thought, as I poured myself a cup of morning coffee. Throughout the day, every time I passed by the flower vase sitting on the kitchen counter, I felt a burst of joy—and a little sadness too as I noted the small dying flower bud. That is why I was surprised the next morning to see a fully blooming rose instead of the wilted bud. Gone was the drooping, pinched-up little bud, and in its place, a fully-opened rose. I bent over and breathed in the roses' rich fragrance as the paper-thin petals caressed my cheek.

Like the rosebud, we humans are fragile and easily crushed. We have no strength within ourselves. Paul admits in 2 Corinthians 12 that he is full of infirmity, with an unnamed, overriding weakness. Just as the roses were severed from their life source, we too face pain and sometimes threatening situations. Sudden difficulties in life often underscore our long-term weaknesses. Our blood pressure goes up; anxiety and depression creep in. Like the wilting rosebud, we struggle to flourish under sudden, overwhelming stress. If we attempt to live in our own strength like roses without water, we will wilt, shrivel up, and die.

However, as Paul says, "Most gladly therefore will I rather glory in my infirmities, that the power of Christ may rest upon me." We blossom only when absorbing the Living Water. If we soak up God's presence, revel in His grace, and abide in His strength, we too can burst into full, fragrant bloom.

The rosebud seemed destined to shrivel up and die. However, its eventual beautiful bloom reminded me that even in our weakness, not despite our brokenness but because of it, we can manifest the fragrance of God's goodness and holiness.

Reflection

Make a list of three things you think are weaknesses in your life and character.

_____

_____

_____

_____

How can you draw your strength from God?

_____

_____

_____

_____

How do you think God can bring glory to Himself through your weaknesses and brokenness?

_____

_____

_____

_____

 Where the Rubber Meets the Road

God turns our greatest weaknesses into His greatest glory.

Day 6

The Divine Mechanic

Scripture Reading: Philippians 4:4-13

Promise from God: I can do all things through Christ which strengtheneth me.

Philippians 4:13 (KJV)

As we climbed a mountain on the interstate, our truck engine was knocking and sputtering, and we were afraid we would not make it to the top. In fact, we were certain our engine was dying. Would our truck leave us stranded on the highway?

Flashback to the summer of 2014. My husband and I had purchased a used truck, a golden oldie, which was all we could afford. Our plan was to take it on the road for summer ministry. My husband and I held vacation Bible schools for smaller churches needing assistance, and we set out on our first road trip after filling our truck with props, games, prizes, and luggage.

However, as we began our journey up the Eastern Seaboard of the United States, it quickly became apparent our truck was using oil, and a lot of it too. Also, we ended up in heavy stop-and-go traffic, which left our truck overheating. After stopping a couple of times to pour several quarts of oil into the engine and a gallon of water into the radiator, we started to wonder if we would reach our destination. The truck was sputtering and belching blue smoke, but we finally made it to our destination in Massachusetts.

After a week of ministry, it was time to start back home. We had no money to have our vehicle checked out, so we decided to travel home on faith. As we climbed into the mountains of Pennsylvania, we were certain our truck was going to die on the interstate, possibly with a blown engine. We decided to pray together out loud on behalf of our vehicle.

As we finished our prayer, the truck started to run more smoothly, and we made it home without incident. Since that trip, we have never had the same difficulties with our truck again. The Divine Mechanic Himself fixed our vehicle. God has brought this experience back to our minds again and again to remind us—we can't work for Him in our own strength. When He gives us a task or job to do, we have learned as a couple we must let God do the work!

Do you ever feel stranded on the road of life? Do you ever feel you are working so hard and making little progress? Sometimes, storms come because of our own mistakes or sins. Other times, we are trying to do God's work with the right motivations, but Satan tries to obstruct our progress.

Ask yourself these questions when faced with a storm. Am I following God's will completely? Is this job or goal dedicated to God? Sometimes roadblocks are signs from God. He uses problems to get our attention. If any part of our heart seeks self-promotion, God will be sure to challenge us to recommit everything to Him. He can use difficulties for His ultimate good.

The only solution, whether a problem is of our own making or whether it is unprovoked, is to let God do the work! Only He can move things in the right direction, giving us the wisdom and strength to overcome obstacles.

Reflection

Describe goals in your life that seem impossible to attain; list jobs or tasks that are overwhelming to you.

_____

_____

_____

_____

How have you tried to overcome obstacles in your own strength?

_____

_____

_____

_____

How can you let God do the work? List three specific steps you are going to take that will help you to rely on God.

_____

_____

_____

_____

 Where the Rubber Meets the Road

When life feels like three steps forward and two steps back, keep in stride with the Master.

Part Three

When I Need Guidance

For from the first day that thou didst set thine heart to understand, and to chasten thyself before thy God thy words were heard, and I am come for thy words.

Daniel 10:12 (KJV)

Day 7

Thy Words
Were Heard

Scripture Reading: Daniel 10:1-21

Promise from God: Then said he unto me, Fear not, Daniel: for from the first day that thou didst set thine heart to understand, and to chasten thyself before thy God, thy words were heard, and I am come for thy words.

Daniel 10:12 (KJV)

L ed captive across the desert as a young man, Daniel understood personal crisis. Cut off from family and childhood friends, his very life in jeopardy, Daniel stayed true to his principles. He gained people's respect because of his character, convictions, and righteousness. Daniel and the lions' den is one of the most famous stories in the Bible. Daniel refused to stop praying to his God three times a day; he threw open his window and bowed his head toward Jerusalem. All his enemies waiting below the window got a full view of his prayer life. We know God was faithful to Daniel in saving him from the lions. God heard his words, and Daniel's personal trauma became an opportunity for God to manifest his glory and power.

Daniel saw prayer as much more than ritual or duty. Several times in the book of Daniel, we read of how he prayed during a crisis. In chapter 2, King Nebuchadnezzar was going to kill all the wise men of Babylon if they could not tell him his dream and its interpretation. Daniel banded together with his three friends, Shadrach, Meshach, and Abednego, for a night of prayer. They were pleading with God for their very lives and the safety of their colleagues. However, their ultimate motive was to bring glory to their God. God responded during their watchful night, which could have been their last one on earth. He revealed the dream and interpretation to Daniel. Daniel praised God for His wisdom, might, and mercy; then he went and witnessed to the

King of God's greatness. Again, while Daniel and his friends suffered, God heard Daniel's words and brought glory to Himself.

As the book closes, Daniel is aging, but he is still praying. God must have been pleased with his life because He reveals more prophecy of future times to Daniel than anyone else in the Bible, other than the Apostle John. Again, Daniel is struggling with an agonizing problem: the ongoing captivity and suffering of his nation. When will they be free? Daniel wants to know. He spends three weeks interceding in a partial fast. But, unlike the night he was with the lions, or the night he was pleading for God to reveal Nebuchadnezzar's dream, God doesn't answer. Daniel's prayers are met with deafening silence. We find out later, from God's Messenger, a battle was raging: a fierce struggle between God's angels and Satan's demons. However, after 21 days, Daniel has a glorious vision.

"Don't be afraid or disheartened. God heard you from the first day of your fasting and praying," the Messenger assures Daniel. "I was prevented from coming, but I am here now. I am come because of your words." Then the Messenger continues to comfort and strengthen Daniel while revealing Divine secrets.

Daniel faced repeated crises and threats throughout his life, but he always responded with prayer. As a result, Satan was repeatedly defeated. Daniel overcame personal suffering, threat of execution, international darkness, and even the demons of Hell through prayer. No simpler formula exists for victory in life. When faced with suffering and threats, pray. When overwhelmed by darkness and evil, pray. The promise of Daniel 10:12 is as relevant in the twenty-first century as it was in 538 B.C.

"Fear not, Daniel: for from the first day that thou didst set thine heart to understand, and to chasten thyself before thy God thy words were heard, and I am come for thy words." In other words, "I was attentive from your first word. I was listening. I was preparing the answer. I am come because of your prayers. Because you held on in faith, because you kept praying until you received an answer, I am now here. I am ready to give you direction. Fear not. Be strengthened. I am your God."

Reflection

What long-term worries or urgent problems do you need God to take care of?

_____

_____

_____

_____

Make a list of three people in your life who need special prayer. How will you pray for them?

_____

_____

_____

_____

When do you have time in your day for sustained and fervent prayer? Record below your regular time for praying. If you do not have one, write down a time you could devote regularly to prayer.

_____

_____

_____

_____

 Where the Rubber Meets the Road

Pray. Pray. Pray. Pray until the answer comes.

Day 8

All These Things

Scripture Reading: Matthew 6:25-34

Promise from God: But seek ye first the kingdom of God, and his righteousness; and all these things shall be added unto you.

Matthew 6:33 (KJV)

As a young teacher, I was laid off from my public-school job due to budget cuts. Two months later, my husband and I were offered jobs at a Christian school. Feeling this ministry opportunity was God's will, we accepted these teaching positions and moved to staff housing on the Christian school campus just one week before school started.

It was not long into the school year we began to hear from other teachers that paychecks could sometimes be delayed. Student tuition did not cover all expenses, and the school relied on donations to operate. A recent recession had hit hard and charitable giving was down, so sometimes teachers continued to do their jobs for weeks without paychecks.

When I was offered a home healthcare job that I could work in the evenings and on weekends, I accepted the position. As it was my husband's first year teaching, he was engulfed in his responsibilities at the school.

Just as we had anticipated, paychecks were delayed as the winter wore on. Several weeks turned into a few months; but with my part-time job, we continued to pay our bills. The school eventually got caught up in payroll, but I was thankful my second job had carried us through the school year.

So, when I was praying one day during the summer, I was taken back when God told me to quit my part-time job.

"Lord," I prayed, "You know how this job has helped us to make ends meet this past school year."

God said, "Yes, but that job is hurting your family. You are away from your husband too much. Quit the job."

I wanted to be obedient to God, and I wanted to be a faithful wife. However, I did struggle with trusting God and giving up the supplemental income. I didn't mean to be arrogant, but I prayed, "I will quit my part-time job, but You will have to pay our bills."

God assured me if I would resign from the job, He would take care of us. I obeyed and gave up the supplemental income.

The next school year, we kept getting letters from the school administrators warning us that paychecks might be late, but those fears never came to fruition. Our paychecks always arrived right on time and have been on time ever since.

Now I'm a stay-at-home mom, and we are totally dependent on one paycheck; however, God always pays our bills.

Sometimes in life we are tempted to look for solutions to our problems all on our own instead of trusting God. We try to pull ourselves out from our difficulties, relying on our own strength. God has promised if we will put His Kingdom first, He will provide for all our needs: "Seek ye first the kingdom of God, and his righteousness; and all these things shall be added unto you."

Reflection

When have you faced a situation of financial or physical need? How was God faithful to you?

_____

_____

_____

_____

What current or future needs do you anticipate? How can you trust God to meet those needs?

_____

_____

_____

_____

"Seek ye first the kingdom of God, and his righteousness; and all these things shall be added unto you." What does this verse mean to you?

_____

_____

_____

_____

Where the Rubber Meets the Road

Have faith that God will be faithful.

Praises at Midnight

Scripture Reading: Acts 16:16-40

Promise from God: And at midnight Paul and Silas prayed, and sang praises unto God: and the prisoners heard them. And suddenly there was a great earthquake, so that the foundations of the prison were shaken: and immediately all the doors were opened, and every one's bands were loosed.

Acts 16:25-26 (KJV)

Blood oozed from their backs. Every breath was an agonizing, pain-filled effort. The stench of human waste assaulted their noses. It was pitch-black. They could hardly see their hands in front of their faces. Perhaps they heard the scurry of little feet. Maybe rats ran over them as they sat forcibly immobile, their feet bound by stocks. Could they have shooed the rodents away, or were their hands also restrained by chains? We don't know.

Paul and Silas had their backs against the wall, literally and figuratively. Satan was laughing and clapping his hands in glee, sure of another victory. And God just waited silently. On the surface, it didn't seem as if Paul and Silas had any efficacy or power to change the situation. However, a spiritual battle raged. Their response would determine the outcome. Would God's servants remain true to Him in spirit, reflecting His holiness? Or would they defect to the Enemy, wallowing in self-pity?

Several hours elapsed. What happened during those hours? Perhaps Paul and Silas were completely silent, except for a few groans. However, hour after hour, they were forced to be still. I imagine both men prayed silently, if not out loud.

By midnight, Paul and Silas were prepared to actively respond to their situation. First, they began to pray, and then they broke out into songs of praise. This was not a quiet activity. They were locked away in the inner prison, perhaps separated from the other prisoners by stone; but the whole jail heard them. God smiled. His servants had come through. They had overcome. God rattled a few rocks; the prison was racked by an earthquake. The doors flew open, and the prisoners' chains fell off.

How can we endure tribulation as Paul and Silas did? How do we gain victory? Just like Paul and Silas, we may not be able to respond immediately to a severe trial or test. We may need some time to recover physically, mentally, and emotionally. During this time of adjustment, we must simply be still before God. We must not gripe, complain, worry, wallow, or despair. In Matthew 24:13, it says, "But he that shall endure unto the end, the same shall be saved."

As we gain strength, praying and singing praises will bring victory. Satan is gleeful when we blame our all-powerful God for allowing our pain. Satan cowers when we respond to our suffering with whole-hearted praise to our Blessed Redeemer.

When facing a dark night, we need to stop and realize we are in a spiritual battle. When wounded, God asks us to be still. Then we should pray. And when we have regained our strength, we must break out into praise. As a result, the demons will be routed, and God will bring clear victory.

Reflection

Acts 16 suggests three steps to victory over suffering: (1.) Be still. (2.) Pray. (3.) Praise. In what stage do you find yourself? How will you keep yourself from complaining or giving up during a trial?

_____

_____

_____

_____

How can you devote yourself to extra prayer time while facing your current problems and difficulties?

_____

_____

_____

_____

When you can't pray your way through, praise your way through. Who has recently heard your testimony to God's goodness? How can you praise God during this time?

_____

_____

_____

_____

 Where the Rubber Meets the Road

When you have been wounded and battered—be still, whisper a prayer, and sing praises—God will transform your trouble.

Part Four

When I Feel Like Giving Up

He will not suffer thy foot to be moved: he that keepeth thee will not slumber.

Psalm 121:3 (KJV)

Day 10

Looking unto the Hills

Scripture Reading: Psalm 121

Promise from God: I will lift up mine eyes unto the hills, from whence cometh my help. My help cometh from the Lord, which made heaven and earth. He will not suffer thy foot to be moved: he that keepeth thee will not slumber.

Psalm 121:1-3 (KJV)

For several years, I have lived in the northern region of the Appalachian Mountains. Two of my homes in the past ten years have been set on the side of a hill, giving me a good view of the mountain ridges flung out on either side.

I enjoy taking nightly walks, sometimes at dusk, other times after the sun has set. Often the sky is clear, and the hills are bathed in moonlight with stars above. Other times, the sky is overcast, and the distant ridges are cloaked in mist with the lights of houses twinkling through the haze. The comforting reality for me is—whether I can see the hills clearly or not, I know they are there. The hills represent safety, security, and home to me. I feel close to God as I walk and pray.

In Psalm 121:1, the Psalmist writes, "I will lift up mine eyes unto the hills, from whence cometh my help." Many scholars believe Psalm 121 was composed by an exile in Babylon. Surrounded by desert plains, the exiled Psalmist looks back to the hills of Israel and ultimately the Temple Mount of Jerusalem, just as the prophet Daniel did when he prayed three times a day. The exiled Psalmist longs for the safety and security of the hills of home, but he also yearns for God—whose presence dwelt in Solomon's Temple on the Temple Mount.

I sometimes cannot see the mountains surrounding my home due to fog or haze, and yet I am comforted by the knowledge that the encircling ridges are there. Through the eyes of faith, the exiled Psalmist sees the hills surrounding Jerusalem and the Temple. The hills are a solid reminder to him of a great God, who brought everything into existence and who is still in total control. The Psalmist reminds himself, "My help cometh from the Lord, which made heaven and earth" (Psalm 121:2). Even though he faces exile, homesickness, and suffering, the Psalmist keeps his eyes upward.

By starting to look up like the exiled Psalmist, we begin to glimpse God. We can speak with God anywhere and at any time, bringing our burdens to Him. However, many times in life, as we face problems and pain, our gaze is constantly fixed downward. When overwhelmed by our own depressed or worried thoughts, it seems safer to stare at the ground as we shuffle along.

God cannot help us if we keep our eyes stubbornly on the obstacles and problems. Our simple choice to look to Him is the first step in beginning to see Him work. Nothing is a surprise to God. He is never caught off-guard. The Psalmist assures himself, "He that keepeth thee will not slumber" (Psalm 121:3). He knows what trouble we will face before we see it ourselves, and He already has the grace to keep us steadfast. "He will not suffer thy foot to be moved" (Psalm 121:3). We need only to ask Him for His strength and help.

Reflection

What have you done to focus on God, rather than fixate on your problems and obstacles?

_____

_____

_____

_____

Develop a specific plan to keep your eyes upward. How will you make looking to God your first response every time stress bears down on you?

_____

_____

_____

_____

Reread Psalm 121. Record below your favorite promise from the Psalm. Consider memorizing this promise or even the entire Psalm.

_____

_____

_____

_____

 Where the Rubber Meets the Road

When everything in your life is on the downward slope, choose to look upward and let God help you, rather than muddle along.

A Photo on the Table

Scripture Reading: I Thessalonians 5:5-24

Promise from God: For God hath not appointed us to wrath, but to obtain salvation by our Lord Jesus Christ, who died for us, that, whether we wake or sleep, we should live together with him. Wherefore comfort yourselves together, and edify one another, even as also ye do.

I Thessalonians 5:9-11 (KJV)

I t was one of those days. I was discouraged. After teaching full time for many years, I was now a stay-at-home mom with a six-week-old baby. I had a good dose of the baby blues, feeling lonely and depressed. My baby suffered from colic and cried frequently, so I held him most of the time throughout the day. As a result, my house was a mess, only compounding my depression. While I knew that nurturing and caring for my infant son was of eternal value, I still felt isolated and cut off from other people. As a teacher, I had enjoyed interacting with teenagers and playing a meaningful role in their lives. I had also appreciated my relationships with co-workers.

"Where are my friends?" I moaned in self-pity to God in prayer. "What am I accomplishing?" Then I spotted it—a wallet-size photo of a former student on the dining room table. Apparently, she had given the picture to my husband, also a teacher, to pass on to me; and he had left it lying on the table. I flipped the portrait over, and read these words: "Mrs. Fritz, thank you for being such an amazing teacher and tutor. Thank you for being my friend and counselor. Keep God #1. I said that because I look up to you as a mentor. Love ya!"

The note kept echoing in my mind throughout the day. I realized my earlier pity party was all about me, not about keeping my Savior first. Instead of pining for my old life, I needed to plunge ahead with what God was calling me to do today—at this very moment! My past work had not been in vain; it was still bearing fruit. I had a new task now—to raise my son, but I was allowing my self-pity to keep me from serving God joyfully.

As Paul says, "For God hath not appointed us to wrath, but to obtain salvation by our Lord Jesus Christ, who died for us, that, whether we wake or sleep, we should live together with him. Wherefore comfort yourselves together, and edify one another, even as also ye do." Christ had died for me. I was enjoying His salvation. I had every reason to rejoice. It was now my responsibility to serve others—to comfort and to edify—just as my former student took the time to comfort me by sending a heart-felt note.

Often, Satan can keep us from focusing on our purpose for today by distracting us with negative emotions. We may feel restless, useless, stressed, lonely, depressed, or over-worked. We become so absorbed in feeling sorry for ourselves that we forget people are watching our lives and hopefully gaining strength from our testimony. We must keep Christ first, not just because He demands it and deserves it, but because we don't live unto ourselves. We are either a witness to God's grace or a distraction from it. As the seasons of our lives change and our responsibilities shift, people are counting on us to stay faithful.

Reflection

List and describe some of the negative emotions you struggle with daily.

_____

_____

_____

_____

Who would you disappoint if you became an unfaithful servant of God?

_____

_____

_____

_____

Write a short prayer below asking God to help you to stay focused on your Divine daily purpose. Ask God to help you manage negative emotions so you can focus on His call for your life.

_____

_____

_____

_____

 Where the Rubber Meets the Road

As Christ-followers, we must keep our eyes on God because others are watching us.

Day 12

Like
Flourishing Trees

Scripture Reading: Psalm 1

Promise from God: And he shall be like a tree planted by the rivers of water, that bringeth forth his fruit in his season; his leaf also shall not whither; and whatsoever he doeth shall prosper.

Psalm 1:3 (KJV)

When my mom and dad married, they built a white brick house on the edge of a hayfield, at the corner of two intersecting roads. They envisioned huge trees sheltering their home, away from buffeting winds and prying eyes of curious passersby. My dad owned an excavating business, and he often did the site preparation for new homes. Sometimes large, full-grown trees would be cut down in preparation for a new building or road. My dad would "rescue" the evergreens—particularly the spruces—digging them up with his earthmoving machines and trucking them home to be transplanted. He would dig large holes in the yard, plop the trees in the holes, and soak the roots with the garden hose.

It became the job of my brother, sister, and me to keep the transplanted trees alive. We would dump brimming buckets of water on these trees—which usually towered above us at 7 or 8 feet. Some of the trees did not make it—their roots had been too severed, or we didn't give them enough water. We would start to see the needles fall. I hated to watch a tree die—a slow and agonizing process. However, often the trees weathered the change—through hot summers—with gallons and gallons of water. My parents still live in their white brick house, but the landscape is changed. The house is no longer visible from the road because the surrounding spruce trees tower 40 and 50 feet into the sky.

Often, in life, we are like those transplanted spruce trees. Life brings many changes, often painful, and our roots are severed. We are transplanted to new situations; we face overwhelming learning curves and periods of adjustment. We sometimes think we will die of emotional and spiritual dehydration. We may thirst for an encouraging word or a refreshing rest. Sometimes when we experience bewildering change, we throw our hands up and say, "I just don't think I can make it." Satan tries to discourage and tempt us to despair. He whispers lies, "God has forgotten about you. God is not going to help you with this new situation. The problems are too big; God could help you, but He probably won't."

Psalm 1 makes some striking promises to those who pursue righteousness—those who are completely surrendered to God's will through the times of transplanting. God not only promises the possibility of acclimation, He promises that "whatsoever" the righteous do "shall prosper." What an elaborate promise, an extravagant guarantee, to grasp onto during the turbulence of change: "And he shall be like a tree planted by the rivers of water, that bringeth forth his fruit in his season; his leaf also shall not whither; and whatsoever he doeth shall prosper" (Psalm 1:3).

Reflection

How do you respond to changes or new seasons in life?

_____

_____

_____

_____

Are you wholly surrendered to God's purpose and will? How are you pursuing righteousness with all your heart?

_____

_____

_____

_____

Reread Psalm 1. Meditate on its truth. How do you see the promise of Psalm 1:3 coming true in your life? How can you see the fulfillment of verse 3 through the eyes of faith?

_____

_____

_____

_____

 Where the Rubber Meets the Road

Despite the transplanting times of this life, we shall flourish for all eternity if we are rooted in God's righteousness.

Part Five

When I Seek Peace

Thou tellest my wanderings: put thou my tears into thy bottle: are they not in thy book? When I cry unto thee, then shall mine enemies turn back: this I know; for God is for me.

Psalm 56:8-9 (KJV)

Day 13

Vials of Tears

Scripture Reading: Psalm 56

Promise from God: Thou tellest my wanderings: put thou my tears into thy bottle: are they not in thy book? When I cry unto thee, then shall mine enemies turn back: this I know; for God is for me.

Psalm 56:8-9 (KJV)

T hroughout history, humans have been fascinated with preserving grief by collecting tears in vials or bottles. In Roman times, during a funeral procession, mourners customarily collected their tears in beautifully-decorated bottles. Sometimes the family of the deceased paid mourners for the number of tears they could collect. These tear bottles were then placed on the grave as a symbol of respect. Victorian times saw the practice renewed. Science had advanced, allowing the creation of bottles with special stoppers, which allowed the tears to evaporate into the air. When the tears were gone, the mourning period was considered over. During the Civil War, some women are said to have collected their tears in bottles after their menfolk marched off to battle. Apparently, it gave these women comfort to collect their tears while they suffered the daily uncertainties and personal tragedies of the most brutal war in United States history.

The custom of collecting tears is also mentioned in the Psalms. In verse 8 of Psalm 56, David asks God to take note of his suffering. "Put thou my tears into thy bottle; are they not in thy book?" David was in miserable, unjust circumstances. King Saul was tracking him down like a tiger stalking prey. In Saul's mind, David threatened his crown; indeed, God had instructed Samuel to anoint David as the next king. However, David had not sought to be king of his own volition, nor had he sought to overthrow Saul. David was facing injustice and possible execution. Homesick, discouraged, and exhausted, David seems to be saying in Psalm 56:8, "Dear God, please don't let my suffering go unnoticed. Count my tears, record them in your book, and collect them in bottles. Don't let my suffering be pointless or wasted."

Sometimes in life's storms, we shed so many tears, we are sure we can't cry any more, but then we do. It is a comfort to know God, who can count the hairs on our head, also sees and keeps track of each teardrop. He knows our sorrow and lives through our pain with us. Jesus also shed tears when He was on this earth, and He intercedes for us to the Father every time we cry.

In fact, as the great Creator, God has designed our physical tears and the act of crying as a path to healing and peace. It's not only okay to cry; it is healthy to cry. Sometimes we are unable to weep physically, but our hearts still cry inwardly. Whether our tears are outward or inward, we can take comfort in the fact God is close to those who have a broken heart.

Reflection

Sometimes we are in too much pain to pray coherently; we can only sob and cry instead. When have you faced a situation in which your prayers melted into tears?

_____

_____

_____

_____

Why are we sometimes afraid to cry?

_____

_____

_____

_____

How do you feel God responds to your tears?

_____

_____

_____

_____

 Where the Rubber Meets the Road

God gave us tears, not to harm us, but to give us a path to healing and peace.

Beneath the Crashing Waves

Scripture Reading: Psalm 42:1-11

Promise from God: He only is my rock and my salvation: he is my defence; I shall not be moved. In God is my salvation and my glory: the rock of my strength, and my refuge, is in God.

Psalm 62:6-7 (KJV)

About 26 miles from Maine's coast, Mount Desert Rock is a barren, soil-less island. Home to one lone lighthouse, this craggy island is exposed to some of the roughest winds and waves of the Eastern Coast. In fact, during storms, Mount Desert Rock is completely submerged in water with only the lighthouse appearing above the waves. For 145 years, humans have tended the lighthouse in this desolate and dangerous spot. Remarkably, though the rocky ground has disappeared in the fiercest tempests and outbuildings have washed away, the lighthouse has remained anchored to the rock. Countless lives—drowning men, women, and children from sinking ships—have been saved by the lighthouse keepers.

The Psalmist in Psalm 42:7 paints a picture analogous to Mount Desert Rock during a storm: "Deep calleth unto deep at the noise of thy waterspouts: all thy waves and thy billows are gone over me." He despairs in verse 9, "I will say unto God my rock, Why hast thou forgotten me?" He can no longer see or feel the Rock. Like an ocean tidal wave crashing over a beleaguered swimmer, fear and despair rush through the Psalmist's soul. His senses are overtaken by a mighty roar; darkness smothers him. However, while doubt threatens to drown him, the Psalmist remembers God, his Rock, is still there, even though he cannot feel Him. He reminds himself over and over: "Why art thou cast down, O my Soul? And why art thou disquieted in me? Hope thou in God." He cannot see God, but the Psalmist recognizes that "in the night his song shall be with me."

In Psalm 62:6-7, the Psalmist says: "He only is my rock and my salvation: he is my defence; I shall not be moved. In God is my salvation and my glory: the rock of my strength, and my refuge, is in God."

Emotional and spiritual agony, depression and anxiety, grief and mental pain—they often come in waves, threatening to drown us. We gulp for air, wondering if we will survive. We know from Scripture and spiritual songs that God is the Rock of our Salvation; but like the Psalmist, we initially wonder, where is God now? Satan taunts us; we lose sight of God amid the tempest.

Peace comes only through a solid resolution to believe God, even when we cannot see or feel the Rock beneath us. Our feelings should become secondary to our faith. Like the Psalmist, we must keep reiterating: "Why art thou cast down, O my Soul? And why art thou disquieted in me? Hope thou in God." We may need to dig up other promises such as Psalm 62:2 to remind us the Rock is still there, "He only is my rock and my salvation: he is my defence; I shall not be greatly moved." Even when we cannot see God, we can hear His song in the night. Even when we do not feel Him, we can know He is there. We will learn our temporal afflictions do not diminish God's lovingkindness; He is still perfectly good, just, and merciful. Through our fiercest storms, we can learn to praise; the crashing waves and billows will no longer erode our peace because through faith we know the Rock is beneath us.

Reflection

How have grief, fear, panic, despair, or sadness overwhelmed you, perhaps crashing over you like waves?

_____

_____

_____

_____

Read Psalm 62. Take time to list several reasons why you can trust the Lord.

_____

_____

_____

_____

How can you cultivate a peace based on faith in God, rather than in fleeting feelings?

_____

_____

_____

_____

 Where the Rubber Meets the Road

When waves of fear and despair crash over my soul, I find peace while resting on the Rock of my Salvation.

Day 15

When God
Says "No"

Scripture Reading: Isaiah 55:6-13

Promise from God: For ye shall go out with joy, and be led forth with peace: the mountains and the hills shall break forth before you into singing, and all the trees of the field shall clap their hands.

Isaiah 55:12 (KJV)

I longed for another child, a sibling for my son. Therefore, I was elated when I discovered shortly before Christmas of 2016 I was expecting again. After years of infertility and a miscarriage, we felt our dreams for a larger family were finally coming true. We would be growing to a family of four.

During week twenty of the pregnancy, we excitedly headed to the doctor's office for the routine ultrasound that usually reveals a baby's gender. However, we left the office shocked and saddened. The ultrasound showed some of our baby's intestines were in his umbilical cord. Further tests revealed more birth defects affecting our unborn son's brain and heart. My precious baby was no longer compatible with life outside the womb. I desperately wanted my son to live; I prayed for a miraculous healing so I could keep my baby.

On a sunny April morning, Aaron David entered the world as a stillborn. His button nose, his rosebud lips, his perfectly-sculpted chest and belly, his tiny arms and legs, and his sweet little feet stole my mama's heart forever. I thought he was so beautiful, and I loved him very much. I had asked God to heal Aaron and let me raise him. However, God decided, "No, My daughter, I'm not going to allow you to keep this child. Your baby will be fully healed, but I'm taking your son to Heaven with Me."

When faced with our own or a loved one's illness, disability, or death, it is easy to ask, "Why is this happening to me? Why not someone else? Why my loved one? Why me?" Personal tragedy comes in so many forms, always taking us by surprise. Many times, there are no logical answers to our questions. Suddenly, the things we don't know outweigh the things we do know. The temptation to stop trusting God creeps over us.

Peace comes when we surrender to God's plan, even when we don't understand it. After marveling at the omniscience, sovereignty, and omnipotence of God in verses 8 to 9, Isaiah goes on to promise in verse 12: "For ye shall go out with joy, and be led forth with peace: the mountains and the hills shall break forth before you into singing, and all the trees of the field shall clap their hands." Surrender is the path to perfect peace and joy.

Our loving Heavenly Father loves to give good gifts to His children, and He feels our anguish when we can't understand His will. He has a higher good in mind, but He knows we as humans are often lost in our temporal pain. Many times, we never know the reason for our suffering. The Divine higher good is beyond our comprehension. In Isaiah 55:8-9, God says, "For my thoughts are not your thoughts, neither are your ways my ways, saith the LORD. For as the heavens are higher than the earth, so are my ways higher than your ways, and my thoughts than your thoughts." God's heart hurts, not only to see us suffer in this sin-cursed world, but because He longs to stop the pain. He does not end our suffering because He knows ultimately what is best for us and for those around us. During a trial, we must release all our pain and grief to God. We can call out, "Oh, God, my heart is breaking. I don't understand why this is happening. Embrace me in my sorrow. Take my anger, my fear, and my sadness. My pain is too heavy for me. Help carry my grief."

A moment by moment reliance on God results in pure peace and joy. To the rational mind, it makes no sense how one can experience tragic loss and still feel a deep, abiding contentment. However, if our faith rests in God, a Divine infusion of peace and joy are promised to us in our deepest seasons of grief: "For ye shall go out with joy, and be led forth with peace."

Reflection

When suffering, we may ask God for a miracle of restoration and healing. Sometimes God says "no" to our most anguished prayer. This is often the hardest response to accept. Complete the following statements to cope with a situation that seems too difficult to understand:

I surrender... _____

_____

I still believe God is... _____

_____

I praise God for... _____

_____

My daily prayer is... _____

_____

I will accept God's peace and joy even though... _____

_____

_____

 Where the Rubber Meets the Road

When God says "no" to our prayers, we can still say "yes" to His will, peace, and joy.

Part Six

When I Lack Courage

The angels of the Lord encampeth round about them that fear him, and delivereth them.

Psalm 34:7 (KJV)

Day 16

Camping
with Angels

Scripture Reading: Psalm 34

Promise from God: The angels of the Lord encampeth round about them that fear him, and delivereth them.

Psalm 34:7 (KJV)

When I was 13, I went on a camping trip with the Girl Scouts. I had never been camping before, and I had rarely stayed overnight by myself without family. We pulled onto the campground at dusk in pouring rain. It had rained all day, and huge puddles had already formed across the campground. The younger girls were staying in cabins, but we older girls were tenting out. As luck would have it, our group was assigned a campsite down in the valley. We pitched our tents, in the darkness and rain, basically in standing water. I tried to settle into my sleeping bag. However, the wind, rain, and thunder—in addition to the moisture seeping into my sleeping bag—did little to make me feel comfortable.

To my young mind, the night was a long one. I was afraid and called out to my best friend, Jesus. He spoke the promise of Psalm 34:7 to my heart, "The angel of the Lord encampeth round about them that fear him, and delivereth them." This promise has echoed in my mind many times over the years when I have faced situations sparking fear or anxiety.

When David penned Psalm 34, he was reflecting on a time when his life was in great danger. Saul was chasing him, so David hid with the Philistines, who then turned on him and plotted to kill him. David couldn't catch a break. He was facing betrayal and danger on all sides; he had nowhere to hide. However, David sensed God was sending His army of angels to surround and protect him. Whether we are afraid of the unknown, as I was as a child on the camping trip, or we face real threats as David did, we can take comfort in the promises of Psalm 34. In verse 4, David goes on to say, "I sought the Lord, and he heard me, and delivered me from all my fears."

Fear is an overwhelming fact of human existence—no one lives very long without experiencing fear. Our "flight or fight" adrenaline response can kick in easily sometimes. However, those who fear and reverence God, do not need to fear anything else. As David says in Psalm 34:9, "O fear ye the Lord, ye his saints: for there is no want to them that fear him."

Banish your fears by claiming the many promises of Psalm 34. Believe David's testimony: "Many are the afflictions of the righteous: but the Lord delivereth him out of them all." David believed the strong, favored, and powerful will come to lack what they need; but those who are wholly dependent on God will never be in want. He says, "The young lions do lack, and suffer hunger; but they that seek the Lord shall not want any good thing."

Reflection

Explain a situation in your life that sparks fear in your heart.

_____

_____

_____

_____

Who in your life fills you with anxiety because of their actions, attitudes, or words? It could be a co-worker, a family member, a friend, an acquaintance, or even a national or political figure.

_____

_____

_____

_____

David knew what it was like to face threatening people or situations. Reread Psalm 34. Contemplate your "Saul" and "Philistine" threats. How you are going to apply the many promises of Psalm 34 to your situation?

_____

_____

_____

_____

 Where the Rubber Meets the Road

Those who fear or reverence God do not need to fear anything else.

Fear Not

Scripture Reading: Isaiah 41:1-13

Promise from God: Fear thou not; for I am with thee: be not dismayed; for I am thy God: I will strengthen thee; yea, I will help thee; yea, I will uphold thee with the right hand of my righteousness.

Isaiah 41:10 (KJV)

I t was late in the evening, and I was getting ready for bed. A thunderous knock sounded on our front door. We lived in a rough and tumble town in Pennsylvania coal country. My husband was the pastor of a small, struggling church. During our two-year tenure at the church, the news frequently carried stories of assaults and occasionally murders, which resulted from local bar room fights and domestic squabbles. Drug and alcohol abuse seemed to fuel the ongoing violence. So, as someone continued to pound on our front door, I was leery about my husband answering it. Most of our parishioners called on the telephone before visiting, and all of them usually came to our back door.

The parsonage was attached to the church, and both buildings opened onto the front street through a small foyer. My husband opened the door of the parsonage. When he looked into the foyer, the front door leading to the street was wide open. No one was there; he glimpsed just an empty sidewalk. The door leading to the church was never locked, and the church was a huge sprawling building, with three different doors connecting to the parsonage. We had a large basement in the building, a fellowship hall, and numerous Sunday school rooms. I had never counted the number of storage rooms, but there were a lot of them. Now, in my frightened mind I pictured an intruder lurking in any one of these rooms or hallways and preparing to break-in to our home, the parsonage. My mind was one note of pure, raw fear.

My husband decided to call the police. A short while later, two officers arrived and searched the church, parsonage, and the property outside for an intruder. During their investigation, they found an abandoned car along the curb and a man passed out on the sidewalk. They thought he was under the influence of some substance and took him into custody. The officers discovered in a background check that the man was a convicted felon, formerly charged with assault and currently on parole.

That night I experienced overwhelming fear, and I was forced to turn to God quickly and completely. Fortunately, the man never entered the open door to our premises. For some reason, he went from manically pounding on our door to passing out in the street gutter. We could have been the victims of a home invasion, maybe even a violent one. However, God had a reason for protecting us; He had a reason for keeping us safe.

Fear is a paralyzing emotion, and it often overtakes us suddenly and with vengeance. However, throughout the Bible, God is clear—we have nothing to fear as His people. In Isaiah 41:10, God says, "Fear thou not; for I am with thee: be not dismayed; for I am thy God: I will strengthen thee; yea, I will help thee; yea, I will uphold thee with the right hand of my righteousness."

What a promise! God begins with two commands: "Fear not" and "Be not dismayed." If we follow these directions, trusting in God's faithfulness, we will begin to feel God's strength, help, and upholding power.

Reflection

Think of a past situation when you were afraid. How did God uphold you, help you, and strengthen you?

_____

_____

_____

_____

How can you trust God to take care of you in the future?

_____

_____

_____

_____

Take time to recopy Isaiah 41:10 below. Then, pray this verse, stopping after each phrase to ask God to make that phrase real in your life.

_____

_____

_____

_____

 Where the Rubber Meets the Road

"Fear not. Be not dismayed."

Day 18

Only Be Still

Scripture Reading: Exodus 14

Promise from God: The Lord will fight for you; you need only to be still.

Exodus 14:14 (NIV)

They are trapped. This sentence conjures up images of people trapped in elevators, underground mines, or flash floods. We envision the accompanying panic and fear. When we are trapped, our most common response is to struggle, fight, or panic. The Israelites in Exodus 14 are facing this range of emotions from hopelessness to overwhelming fear. After leaving Egypt, they approach the Red Sea. Suddenly, through a cloud of dust, the people see Pharaoh's army coming after them. Moreover, God has led them into this corner with the cloud-like pillar.

I can see the people gathered: grandparents, aunts, uncles, moms, and dads. The adults are straining to see and asking those around them if they know what is going on. The children are huddled around, clinging to the adults' clothing as they sense the pervading fear. Then Moses rises up and assures the people that the Lord will fight for them—they "need only to be still." In other words, don't panic. God will perform a miracle, just sit back and watch. For many of the people, if not most, this is an almost impossible task. Don't panic! What do you mean, don't panic? An entire army is pounding across the desert, and we are about to be massacred with our children.

Scholars believe the children of Israel were trapped between two mountains with the Red Sea before them. They were facing almost certain death, or at the very least re-enslavement. We all know what happens over the course of the next few hours. God literally makes a road through the sea, allows all His children to pass through, and lures the Egyptians to their deaths—a huge wall of water crashing over them as they try to follow the Israelites.

What would have happened if the children of Israel had panicked and failed to heed Moses' command? We can think of many possibilities. The children, elderly, and disabled could have been killed in a human stampede as people tried to run to safety. Or maybe individuals running in shock would have become separated from the group, eventually dying of hunger and thirst all alone in the wilderness. The command "only be still" had to be obeyed so every individual could safely make it through the Red Sea. Fortunately, the Israelites obeyed God's instructions and were delivered.

God did not just command the children of Israel to be still. An often-quoted Scripture, "Be still, and know that I am God" (Psalm 46:10), applies to everyone. When faced with a situation beyond our control, God asks us to "be still" and let Him handle the outcome.

Reflection

Why do we as humans often panic when faced with a fearful situation?

_____

_____

_____

_____

While you cannot predict how God will work (after all, He is full of surprises), how do you believe God will bring glory to Himself through your storm?

_____

_____

_____

_____

How can you "be still" before God about the outcome?

_____

_____

_____

_____

Where the Rubber Meets the Road

When our prayers consist of "Why?" and "But," God says, "Be still."

Part Seven

When I Long for Love

For ye have not received the spirit of bondage again to fear; but ye have received the Spirit of adoption, whereby we cry, Abba, Father.

Romans 8:15 (KJV)

Day 19

Abba, Father

Scripture Reading: Romans 8:12-17

Promise from God: For ye have not received the spirit of bondage again to fear; but ye have received the Spirit of adoption, whereby we cry, Abba, Father.

Romans 8:15 (KJV)

"**D**addy! Daddy! Daddy!" The voices of excited children drifted towards me on the early evening breeze. I glanced up to see the neighbors' children rushing across their yard. Their father was arriving home from work. As soon as he had parked his truck, the children rushed to their dad, ready to hug him as he opened his truck door.

Several months later, the children's voices breathless with love and gladness over the arrival of their father still echo in my mind. I squirm a little as the Holy Spirit convicts me. Do I greet my Heavenly Father with such anticipation and exhilaration? In prayer, do I cry out "Daddy! Daddy!" or "Abba, Father"?

Our God longs to be our daddy. He wants us to revel in His unconditional love. When we feel unlovable, He wants us to find our value in Him. When others exclude and injure us, He wants us to run to His arms. He wants to affirm us when others degrade us. He desires to be our Sustainer, our Protector, and our Champion.

I think God knew, in this sin-cursed world, many human fathers would fail, hurt, or reject their children. If we have an absent, indifferent, or abusive earthly father, it may be hard to understand or believe in the unmitigated goodness and love of our Heavenly Father. We may struggle to connect or delight in the presence of God, if our earthly father has walked away or injured us. In fact, the very term "father" may cause us to recoil in horror. Some people endure a lifetime of painful memories related to their father—a storm of emotions always rumbles in the background. Beneath every joyful experience or happy celebration is a scab or even an open wound of pain.

God longs to redeem fatherhood and restore it to its pre-Fall, pristine innocence—the Father in His perfection and goodness takes on the term Himself. Paul says, "For as many as are led by the Spirit of God, they are the sons of God. For ye have not received the spirit of bondage again to fear; but ye have received the Spirit of adoption, whereby we cry, Abba, Father" (Romans 8:14-15). The bondage, the fear, the lovelessness of our past—God redeems with His unconditional, grace-filled love.

In return, God longs to hear us cry out, "Abba, Father." Our childlike adoration and affection warm His heart. "Daddy! Daddy! Daddy! I love you."

Reflection

Jot down or sketch your image of an ideal father—one way to do this is to make a list of five traits you believe a father should possess.

_____

_____

_____

_____

How have earthly fathers disappointed you in these ideals?

_____

_____

_____

_____

Take time to find Scriptures that reveal our Heavenly Father's nature. List some of these Scripture references below. Meditate on these Scriptures and ask God to show Himself to you.

_____

_____

_____

_____

 Where the Rubber Meets the Road

No one need be fatherless—our Heavenly Father opens His arms. Fall into His embrace.

Day 20

Junk Mail

Scripture Reading: Matthew 5:38-48

Promise from God: But I say unto you, Love your enemies, bless them that curse you, do good to them that hate you, and pray for them which despitefully use you, and persecute you; That ye may be the children of your Father which is in heaven: for he maketh his sun to rise on the evil and on the good, and sendeth rain on the just and on the unjust.

Matthew 5:44-45 (KJV)

I groaned inwardly as I passed by the kitchen counter. I had left a pile of junk mail lying there. After getting the mail earlier in the day, my son needed my attention, and I did not take time to shred and throw away the four or five envelopes and flyers. A couple of credit card offers, a product advertisement, and a membership promotion were in the pile: useful things in themselves. However, I didn't currently need any of these things, so the envelopes were just junk mail.

For me, junk mail is a constant irritant. As a busy mom, every minute is precious. I resent the daily time I must spend sorting, shredding, and throwing away this unwanted mail. The junk mail situation caused me to contemplate other daily irritants building up in my life. These situations so often bring me down emotionally and spiritually; I began to pray that God would help me to deal with these other "junk mail" experiences.

We all face our own "junk mail" moments. Consider a few of these and take note of any that exist in your own life: a friend whose daily or weekly complaining and "venting" sessions leave you exhausted; a spouse who makes random sarcastic or nagging comments that gradually wear you down; a parent who continues to criticize you throughout your adulthood, finding fault with everything you do; or a child who constantly melts down or argues with you (could be a toddler or a teenager!). Other common "junk mail" situations include people who assault others regularly with their worry-statements, the people who insinuate they are superior to others, or the people who are always making excuses for letting others down.

A common refrain of popular self-help advice is to rid your life of toxic people. The reality is often our family members and life-long friends bring emotional junk into our lives, and we can't just throw our loved ones away. Neither should we push away broken, hurting people. Jesus said, "Love your enemies, bless them that curse you, do good to them that hate you, and pray for them which despitefully use you." He goes on to add that God is merciful to all—evil, good, just, and unjust. He blesses us all with rain and sunlight.

The only solution to coping with "junk mail" in this sin-cursed world is to turn these daily irritants over to God. Sometimes we do need to separate ourselves from emotionally or verbally abusive people. However, in most cases, we can simply take the "junk mail" words that come our way and hand them over to our Father. When confronted with a negative or difficult interaction, we can develop the habit of immediately praying, "God, take this complaint, criticism, or worry. Help me to respond peaceably and with joy." When our immediate impulse is to turn to God, He helps us not to internalize the negative attitudes or words being passed on to us. And the people we interact with may be positively changed by our peaceful and calming response.

Reflection

Make a list of toxic or "junk mail" situations that regularly build up in your life.

_____

_____

_____

_____

Reread Matthew 5:44-45. What promise is extended to those who respond to difficult people with Christ-like behavior?

_____

_____

_____

_____

How can you triumph emotionally and spiritually over "junk mail" in your life?

_____

_____

_____

_____

 Where the Rubber Meets the Road

When you feel targeted by "junk mail" with no opportunity to "opt-out," hand the situation over to God and leave it with Him.

Day 21

Never Alone

Scripture Reading: John 14:15-21

Promise from God: Even the spirit of truth; whom the world cannot receive, because it seeth him not, neither knoweth him: but ye know him; for he dwelleth with you, and shall be in you. I will not leave you comfortless: I will come to you.

John 14:17-18 (KJV)

During tenth grade, I attended a small Christian high school in Canada. It turned out to be a difficult year for me. I was a gangly girl with a chronic acne breakout, large round eyeglasses, and unusually long hair that I wore in a braid. Due to my faith, I never wore pants, makeup, or jewelry like other teenage girls. My appearance along with my preoccupation with books and grades made me an easy target. After enduring a lot of snide comments and mocking laughter, I would often disappear to the bathroom, stare into the mirror, and will myself to get through my school day. Sometimes, I would enter a classroom with the gouges of nail prints in my hands, I was clenching my fists so hard, telling myself, "I can get through this school day. I can make it."

I took refuge in learning and studying, finding affirmation and encouragement from my teachers. I particularly loved history and social studies, which was why I was very excited when our teacher announced a field trip to the Canadian Parliament buildings in Ottawa. I had always wanted to see my nation's capital. On the morning of my greatly anticipated adventure, the students loaded up into two large vans. I happened to be grouped with the same girls who had harassed me all year. One boy, whom I will call Sam, was also assigned to our van; he too had been socially ostracized by the other teens. As our van headed out on the highway, I was determined to have a good day and not let the bullies bother me.

Unfortunately, the teacher driving our van did not have a good sense of direction and got lost in the city of Ottawa. In those pre-GPS days, her wrong turn was not easily sorted out. We drove aimlessly around for a while, before the teacher decided we had missed our tour of the Parliament buildings anyway, so we might as well just meet up with the rest of the group on the edge of the city before heading home. The teacher then decided to take us to the mall to kill some time while we waited for the other van to catch up with us. Tears of disappointment welled in my eyes; the field trip I had so anticipated was ruined.

The teacher sent us students to explore the mall on our own. The other girls did not want to be seen in public with me or with Sam. Soon, the girls ditched us by jumping on an elevator, leaving me alone with Sam, a boy I hardly knew. As I watched the girls in the glass elevator shoot up to the fourth floor without me, I felt rejected, alone, and worthless. I spent a long afternoon in a strange city mall, deeply hurt and disappointed. Today, I can't recall this experience, and my entire sophomore year of high school, without pain and sadness.

Feelings of isolation and rejection are a heartsickness some carry with them for life. One experience of being ostracized can lead to deep and lasting pain. However, something I learned in high school is while humans may reject me, God is always with me. Jesus assured His disciples in verses 17 and 18 of John 14 that after He ascended back into Heaven God would send the Holy Spirit, who would dwell always with His followers: "Ye know him; for he dwelleth with you, and shall be in you. I will not leave you comfortless: I will come to you." As a lonely girl in a high school bathroom, I felt the Holy Spirit responding to my prayers. I knew I was not alone. In a strange city with abandoning school mates, I learned God was always with me. Throughout my high school years, when I cried out to God, I knew He was there.

And all through life, I have never been alone. God has always been with me. And so He always is, with all those who love Him and keep His commandments. We are never alone.

Reflection

Describe a time when you have felt lonely.

_____

_____

_____

_____

Why does God sometimes allow us to feel alone?

_____

_____

_____

_____

How can we find comfort through God's Word and the presence of the Holy Spirit?

_____

_____

_____

_____

 Where the Rubber Meets the Road

Though humans desert and hurt us, God is always with us.

Part Eight

When I Need Comfort

Like as a father pitieth his children, so the Lord pitieth them that fear him.

Psalm 103:13 (KJV)

Day 22

"Be Calm, Little One"

Scripture Reading: Psalm 103

Promise from God: Like as a father pitieth his children, so the Lord pitieth them that fear him.

Psalm 103:13 (KJV)

W hen my son was a baby, he did not like to be left alone. He could be happily playing with toys on the floor, and if I stepped out of the room for even a minute, he would burst out crying. I frequently would use the phrase "Be calm, Little One" to comfort him.

I still use "Be calm, Little One" from time to time now that my son is a toddler. Speaking with a gentle tone, I attempt to assure the hungry, tired, thirsty, or restless child that things are going to be better soon. What I mean in saying "Be calm, Little One" is I care about your problems, my child. I'm not going to let you go hungry, thirsty, or tired for much longer. I'm working on getting you a bottle or a drink. I'm changing your diaper so you can go down for a nap. "Be calm, Little One." Mama hears your discomfort, and I will make it all right.

Like a loving parent, God too assures and comforts His people. God promises the children of Israel in Isaiah 66:13, "As one whom his mother comforteth, so will I comfort you." In Psalm 103:13, the Psalmist declares, "Like as a father pitieth his children, so the Lord pitieth them that fear him." God says to us, "You are my child. You are precious to Me."

As our sovereign God, He has everything under control. When we are anxious about the future, God says, "Rest in Me." On a planet racked by mudslides, tsunamis, earthquakes, and floods, God says, "Be not afraid." In a world marked by violence, riots, wars, political upheaval, and terrorism, God says, "Be calm, Little One."

Only God's all-powerful, loving nature can bring us comfort in tempestuous times. When we don't understand why, God says, "Trust

Me." When the circumstances of our life overwhelm us, God says, "I'm in control." When we hurt, when we think we will give way under the pain, when we don't know how we can go on in our suffering, God says, "Be calm, Little One."

We can trust completely in God's providence. He is our resting place. When others mistreat and hurt us, God says, "I love you." When unkind things are said to our face or behind our back, God says, "I am your Defender." When we are judged harshly and our Christianity is unjustly called into question, God says, "Be calm, Little One."

God's mercy, grace, and love are boundless. When we have sinned, God says, "I forgive." When Satan tries to accuse us, God says, "You are redeemed." When our personal failures pile up, when guilt over the past weighs us down, when we feel so inadequate, God says, "Be calm, Little One."

As our loving Father, God never ignores our cries. He always responds to us. We need only listen for His comforting assurances.

Reflection

What problems or worries are overwhelming you today?

_____
_____
_____
_____

How can you take comfort in the promises of Psalm 103? Reread this Psalm and list the promises that give you peace.

_____
_____
_____
_____

How do you believe God is saying "Be Calm, Little One" to you today? How will you let Him speak to you and calm your spirit?

_____
_____
_____
_____

 Where the Rubber Meets the Road

Just as a baby nestles in the arms of a parent, rest in the hands of God today.

Day 23

The Parable
of the Diamond

Scripture Reading: II Corinthians 4:5-18

Promise from God: For our light affliction, which is but for a moment, worketh for us a far more exceeding *and* eternal weight of glory; While we look not at the things which are seen, but at the things which are not seen: for the things which are seen *are* temporal; but the things which are not seen *are* eternal.

II Corinthians 4:17-18 (KJV)

I n Africa, a diamond was sifted from the sands. The old man who found the diamond had devoted a lifetime to searching for the most valuable gem in the world. Most of his finds had been small diamonds—they often weighed less than a carat—bringing in only a few dollars. However, although this stone was opaque and there was no way to determine what imperfections it might have at its heart, the old man had a feeling this diamond was the find of a lifetime. It was the size of a bar of soap; and when he took it to the diamond buyers, it weighed over 250 carats. The old man was rich—he had harvested a legacy.

The diamond made its way through the world's gem markets and was purchased by a New York jeweler. In a midtown Manhattan, heavily-guarded workroom, the jeweler handed the diamond in the rough over to his master cutter. The cutter studied the diamond through his loupe, or magnifying glass. He had a good eye for figuring how to perfectly cut a diamond from the stone with minimal waste. By instinct, he could often determine just the size and shape to cut from the rough stone to produce a beautiful, awe-inspiring diamond.

The master diamond cutter made the first incision in the stone. His heart beat with excitement—there was potential for purity within the heart of this diamond; it needed only to be properly cut and polished.

The work would take several weeks, if not months; but the master diamond cutter sat down at his cutting wheel with determination. He would patiently polish this diamond until it was flawless by placing it on a scaife, a wheel covered in oil and diamond dust that polishes a diamond one fine layer at a time as the wheel spins round and round.

Some diamonds cry out in pain and resistance when clamped on the polishing wheel or scaife. But not this diamond; it meekly yielded to the master's wheel. The diamond did not cry out. Hours, days, weeks passed by—the diamond continued to spin; the master cutter continued to shape the stone with dozens of facets, which would radiate light from both the surface and the heart of the diamond.

Like most diamonds, there was no clue as to where this gem originated—it was completely independent of its past. The diamond's sooty origins were completely erased. And so, this rough stone originating in the sandy diamond pits of the Congo became one of the world's largest oval-cut diamonds—completely flawless.

Just like the diamond, which begins as a clump of carbon—the same material as coal—we too are born in sin. Through tremendous pressure and heat, the diamond appears in the gut of the earth like an ulcer. We too grow into adulthood affected by the ravages of the curse, but God in His sovereignty allows us to be rescued from the pit of sin. Just as the old man found the diamond, God sends Christ-followers to harvest sinful men, women, and children. We come to God in the rough—ugly stones—which other humans often see as worthless.

However, after our salvation from sin, Christ, the master diamond-polisher, puts us—His diamonds in the rough—on His polishing wheel. Those who cry out in complaint to the cutting and the polishing are destined to be imperfect. However, those who sweetly yield their all to the cutting—those diamonds can be polished to perfection.

The word diamond comes from the Greek word for "unbreakable." Sometimes we may feel as if we are going to shatter into a million pieces under the pain and pressure of the Master's scaife, but God has designed our trials to make us strong, beautiful, and precious. Without affliction, we are useless to God. Paul said, "For our light affliction, which is but for a moment, worketh for us a far more exceeding and eternal weight of glory."

God uses serious suffering and everyday stress in our lives to form us into His diamonds. The troubles we face will eventually melt away when time is abolished, but the diamond remaining in our souls will last for all of eternity.

Reflection

When faced with affliction, how can we keep our hearts from becoming cold, hard, or bitter?

_____
_____
_____
_____

What beautiful qualities do you see God forming in your life? For example, have your troubles taught you to be more grateful, patient, and empathetic?

_____
_____
_____
_____

Finish this thought: I praise God for polishing me into a beautiful and useful gem. I feel He is bringing glory to Himself through me because _____

_____
_____
_____

 Where the Rubber Meets the Road

When we feel the pressure and heat, God is forging a diamond. When we feel the cut of the blade, God is creating a jewel. Trust the Master Gem-maker.

Day 24

Just as I Am

Scripture Reading: John 6:26-40

Promise from God: All that the Father giveth me shall come to me; and him that cometh to me I will in no wise cast out.

John 6:37 (KJV)

C harlotte Elliot was bedridden for 50 years. In her early 30s, Elliot was stricken with a debilitating illness, which left her weak and unable to function normally. Remarkably, she lived to age 82. During those five decades of chronic disease, Charlotte penned many hymns and poems, which she published in two separate books.

From a family of devout Christians, many of Charlotte's relatives were clergymen or active in Christian service. Partly due to her illness, Charlotte felt useless and inferior. At first, she felt she might not be worthy of salvation. A visiting minister from another country assured her that she must come to God, "just as you are." Those words opened Charlotte's eyes to the truth of redemption, and she asked the Lord Jesus to forgive her sin and to reside in her heart.

The phrase "just as you are" stuck with Charlotte for many years. It came back to her mind when she was again struggling with low self-worth. Her family was planning a fundraiser for Christian ministry. Charlotte's uncle was starting a Christian school for girls, and Charlotte's family was planning a bazaar to raise funds. While everyone was bustling about, preparing for the event, Charlotte wondered what use she was to God. Confined to her room, she recalled the words "just as you are," and she began penning the hymn "Just as I Am." She realized in God's eyes she was not inferior or unworthy, but that God loved her just as she was. When she published her poem "Just as I Am," she included John 6:37 under the title: "Him that cometh to me I will in no wise cast out." Those words, coupled with the hymn, have led countless souls to salvation, and the hymn continues to encourage believers.

Just like Charlotte, you too may suffer from a lifelong illness or disease. Racked by chronic pain or fatigue, you may feel you are virtually worthless in the Kingdom of God. Do not despair. Perhaps in your suffering, God has some ministry for you, just as He did for Charlotte. The words "Just as I Am" have been instrumental in leading many people to Christ. If Charlotte had been able-bodied, perhaps she would have never penned those words because she would have been participating in the fundraiser instead of praying and writing in her bedroom.

We should never allow Satan to convince us our problems and limitations make us useless to God or inferior as people. Remember, God has a purpose for everything happening in our lives as it says in Romans 8:28: "All things work together for good to those who are called according to his purpose." All trials and problems originate in the evil of this sin-cursed world, but God uses our suffering to refine us.

Many times, when faced with physical or emotional problems that leave us feeling run-down and depressed, it is easy to lock the doors of our home, pull the blinds down, and throw a pity party for ourselves. However, Charlotte Elliot inspires us to find our self-worth and purpose in God. If we will let Him, He will bring glory to Himself through our pain. He will build His Kingdom, drawing souls to Himself, because of our suffering. Claim the precious promise of John 6:37, just as Charlotte did, "Him that cometh to me I will in no wise cast out." Trust God. Trust His purpose.

Reflection

Relate a time you struggled to find God's purpose in your life. How did God show you His will?

_____

_____

_____

_____

How can feelings of self-pity or inferiority interfere with your effectiveness for God?

_____

_____

_____

_____

How do you feel unworthy, inferior, or useless? List some of your feelings below. Then bow your head, releasing your emtoions to God, one by one.

_____

_____

_____

_____

 Where the Rubber Meets the Road

God asks us to come to Him just as we are—so He can make us into what He would have us to be.

Part Nine

When I Crave Hope

Now unto him that is able to do exceeding abundantly above all that we ask or think, according to the power that worketh in us, Unto him be glory in the church by Christ Jesus throughout all ages, world without end. Amen.

Ephesians 3:20-21 (KJV)

Day 25

Symmetrical Feet

Scripture Reading: Ephesians 3:14-21

Promise from God: Now unto him that is able to do exceeding abundantly above all that we ask or think, according to the power that worketh in us, Unto him *be* glory in the church by Christ Jesus throughout all ages, world without end. Amen.

Ephesians 3:20-21 (KJV)

When our first son was born, we loved him at first sight. However, we soon noticed he had a twisted foot. With kindness and compassion, the hospital pediatrician told us he suspected our beautiful baby had a club foot, and he referred us to a specialist. A week later, we had a definite diagnosis of club foot. At four weeks, our son began a rigorous treatment schedule. His little foot and leg were encased in a plaster cast designed to straighten his foot. Every week the old cast was removed and a new one was put on. Little by little, our son's foot was bent back into the correct position. This resulted in days of discomfort during which he cried often and refused to eat. As new parents, we agonized over our son's apparent pain and his nutrition. After several weeks and seven casts, our son then underwent surgery on his foot to treat his Achilles tendon, followed by another three weeks in a leg cast. We held our son a lot during his three months of treatment and prayed over him. We were thankful the birth defect was treatable and it was not going to impact his quality of life in future years. Yes, he did have to wear special boots and a brace to bed every night for the first four years of his life; but he learned to walk, run, and play with a normal gait.

From his birth, I prayed that God would touch Isaiah's feet according to His will. Remarkably, God did allow Isaiah's feet to heal beyond my expectations. Many children with one club foot have different size feet, leg lengths, or leg calves. Usually, the calf of the club foot is thinner than the healthy leg, and the club foot can be different in size, sometimes two or three shoe sizes in difference. Also, one leg can be longer than the other. I accepted these facts and never once did I pray for Isaiah's feet to be symmetrical, and yet God chose to heal our son's legs and feet so they were virtually identical in size. At Isaiah's one year appointment, his medical team was amazed by the symmetry of his feet and legs. We thanked God for this blessing, knowing many children with a club foot never experience this complete healing.

When I cradle my son's little feet, I think of how God transforms our broken, sin-marred lives. At birth, our hearts are already disfigured by sin, a universal birth defect. As we grow and make decisions, we too often make the wrong ones, and our souls become cracked and splintered with moral corruption. However, God not only forgives; He can restore our souls completely. He can take our twisted, weak, and gnarled lives and make us beautiful, whole, and complete.

Isaiah's feet also remind me of Paul's prayer to the Ephesians. Paul is praying for spiritual blessings upon them. He asks God to strengthen the Ephesians by His Holy Spirit. He also prays they will be rooted and grounded in love, they will know the fullness of Christ's love, and they will be filled with all the fullness of God. He acknowledges our great God will do all this and more because He "is able to do exceeding abundantly above all that we ask or think" (Ephesians 3:20). In His love, God always does what is best for us. He is not only able, but He continually does "exceeding abundantly above all that we ask or think." When He withholds physical blessing, He does it in love. When He pours out physical blessing, He does it also in love.

I never imagined my son's feet would be restored as they were; I never even thought to pray his feet and legs would be symmetrical. God did exceedingly and abundantly above what I could ask or think .

Reflection

Describe a time when God's answer to your prayers exceeded your expectations.

_____

_____

_____

_____

Explain your current needs. How have you presented these problems or desires to God?

_____

_____

_____

_____

Complete this thought: I believe God "is able to do exceeding abundantly above all that we ask or think" because

_____

_____

_____

_____

 Where the Rubber Meets the Road

When walking with God, expect the unexpected. God knows best.

Day 26

When Love Doesn't Seem to Be Enough

Scripture Reading: Luke 15: 11-32

Promise from God: For this thy brother was dead, and is alive again; and was lost, and is found.

Luke 15:32 (KJV)

For a long time, they looked like the perfect family. You know the type—the family that regularly posts pictures on social media with members wearing color-coordinated outfits. They didn't seem to have financial troubles, and they went on splendid vacations. Everyone in the family seemed to get along—no hint of marital discord or sibling rivalry.

Then things started to fall apart. No mother is mentioned in the parable of Luke 15, so she may have died because of childbirth or disease. The father soldiers on with his two sons. His farm and business pursuits go well. However, as the boys mature into manhood, the seams of the family unravel. The younger son demands his inheritance, creating a family rift. Then he disappears. He squanders his money, and he eventually finds himself at the bottom, literally in a pig pen.

Let's consider this story from the perspective of the father. For some time after his son left, perhaps many years, he did not know what had happened to his boy. Maybe he heard of the famine and assumed the worst. For a while, perhaps the father blamed himself for how his son had turned out, waking up every morning with a fresh dose of hurt and sadness. The question of what he should do to reach out to his son probably haunted him every day. Should he set out and look for the prodigal? Through it all, he never stopped loving his son.

Only those who have experienced the estrangement of a loved one will be able to truly understand this man's pain. Unfortunately, the very existence of love means every human has the free will to reject love. Perhaps you have a spouse, sibling, child, niece, nephew, or grandchild who has walked away from the love of family. Their choices whether willful or caused by mental illness can be very difficult to understand. Drug abuse, relationship abuse, alcoholism, sexual addiction, gambling, and other problems may have so taken over your loved one that you hardly recognize him or her any more. You may have had to make some tough choices. Like the father in this story, you may sleep fitfully, only to awake each morning with the searing pain of your loved one's estrangement rushing in upon you again. Is there any hope, you ask yourself? There are no easy answers to this question, but the story in Luke 15 can serve as a beacon of hope to any person facing a similar situation. The son, from the father's perspective, returns from the dead: "Thy brother was dead, and is alive again; and was lost, and is found."

When situations look the bleakest, we can find hope in God's unfailing love. When human love doesn't seem to be enough, God's love can redeem broken lives and heal estranged relationships. Place your hope in the fact that God loves our loved ones more than we ever could. Keep trusting God.

Reflection

How have you felt the pain of estrangement or the scars of another's sinful choices?

_____

_____

_____

_____

How will you cultivate the faith that God's unfailing love will reach your loved one?

_____

_____

_____

_____

Insert the name of a lost loved one in the following promise: "For _____ was dead, and is alive again; and was lost, and is found." Pray over this promise, asking God to bring salvation and restoration to the life of your loved one.

 Where the Rubber Meets the Road

When your love doesn't seem to be enough to help a lost soul, remember no sinner is beyond the reach of Christ's love.

Day 27

Deadly Rain

Scripture Reading: Psalm 147:1-11

Promise from God: He healeth the broken in heart, and bindeth up their wounds.

Psalm 147:3 (KJV)

It was one of the costliest natural disasters in Canadian history and involved the largest peace-time deployment of the military. Over 30 people lost their lives. And it all began with a few raindrops. In January 1998, a powerful storm system developed over Ontario and Quebec, Canada, and the northern United States. As a teenager living with my family in Ontario, I don't remember being concerned when the rain began to fall. In that region of North America, freezing rain is a common winter phenomena—rain falls in sub-freezing temperatures, building up ice on all outside surfaces. What made this storm unique is that the freezing rain lasted for days. Everything—trees, cars, homes, powerlines, and the ground—was soon covered in inches of ice.

I still remember the night when the trees surrounding our house could hold no more weight. Lying in bed with the windows and doors shut, I could hear thousands of limbs and trees crashing down, no longer able to hold the ice. I opened the door in the middle of the night—a constant cacophony greeted my ears, as if thousands of crystal chandeliers were crashing to the ground.

Then we were plunged into darkness when the electricity went out. The next several days and nights were cold and dark as we had to survive without electrical power. The high-transmission power line towers that carried electricity across the region twisted and bowed under the burden of the ice, toppling like dominos, and wiping out electricity to millions of people for several days and weeks. Our family was better off than many as we had a wood stove and access to a generator.

The storm's impact on the forests was incredible—devastating trees and bushes. Orchards and sugar maple trees were hard hit. Looking at some of those trees, maimed and missing so many limbs, I wondered how these trees would ever be the same. However, spring did come again. The trees budded, the bark grew, and little by little the scars begin to disappear. Now twenty years later, while walking through the woods, I can no longer see the damage of the ice storm of 1998. The trees have been restored. Certainly, there are scars deep within the trees' trunks. An experienced arborist would probably be able to spot the damage of the storm in the trees' growth rings. However, the trees that survived the storm have healed—today they are thriving. Looking at those trees a week after the ice storm, it was hard to picture their future—their limbs stripped, the bark ripped open, and the trunks bent. However, many of those trees not only survived, they are flourishing today.

Just as God has given trees a remarkable ability to weather storms, He is ready to heal and restore His children when we are battered by life. In Psalm 147:3, the Psalmist proclaims, "He healeth the broken in heart, and bindeth up their wounds." Trouble, suffering, and affliction leave us damaged—our emotions in tatters, our bodies tired, and our minds trying to sort out what has happened to us. However, God is ready to bind up our wounds and heal our broken hearts, if we will turn to Him. Through His Word and His Holy Spirit, God can take our maimed lives—our shattered hearts and wounded spirits—and heal and restore them.

During a storm, I often find myself thinking, "I'm never going to be the same again after this." And as I begin to emotionally and mentally assess the damage to my life, I wonder how I will pick up the many pieces. How will I ever be whole again? The damage seems too great. However, in reading God's Word and in studying His creation, it quickly becomes apparent to me that God specializes in restoring broken things. He can help us to not only survive life's storms—but to triumph over them and to flourish.

Reflection

What damage have you sustained from your life's storms?

_____

_____

_____

_____

Reread Psalm 147:3. How can you find hope in this promise?

_____

_____

_____

_____

Complete this thought: I know God can restore my brokenness and help me to flourish because _____

_____

_____ .

 Where the Rubber Meets the Road

Time does not heal all wounds—God does.

Day 28

Waiting for
the Rainbow

Scripture Reading: Romans 8:12-31

Promise from God: And we know that all things work together for good to them that love God, to them who are the called according to his purpose.

Romans 8:28 (KJV)

F or several weeks, it rained almost every day—sometimes just a sudden shower or two. On other days, the sun didn't come out at all. A few times, it rained even when the sun was shining. One afternoon as the raindrops came filtering down through the sunlight, I rushed outside to see if I could spot a rainbow. I scanned the sky, but all I could see were clouds. I was growing tired of the rainy weather. I was caring for two foster children in addition to my own little boy— three children, ages four and under. The children were growing restless because they couldn't play outside. I felt emotionally down.

Then one day, it happened. All the conditions needed for a beautiful rainbow came together. It arched high in the sky—a full bow of color— extending from the southern to the northern horizon. On that stormy afternoon, some of my friends and neighbors even saw a double rainbow; and pictures quickly appeared on social media. I had waited for a rainbow for days, and I was not disappointed. The experience reminded me of verse 25 of Romans 8, "But if we hope for that we see not, then do we with patience wait for it." I waited expectantly for a rainbow, and I was ready to run outside to scan the sky for one. This is the kind of hope God wants us to have in our lives, one of positive expectation.

Many of us must deal with chronic and ongoing problems that steal our hope. In other words, we don't see sunlight for days. Some face sickness and illness, bodies racked with daily pain and discomfort.

95

Sometimes we are weary in spirit. Our marriages may be struggling. Maybe problems have arisen in other family relationships: a parent's health is declining or a child has become wayward. Maybe our job situation has steadily worsened; we are worried about our livelihood. Maybe we are just restless and dissatisfied with our daily life, and we are not sure why.

Paul describes our sin-corrupted world in Romans 8:21-23. He says, "For we know that the whole creation groaneth and travaileth in pain together until now." He goes on to acknowledge even Christians struggle with the curse of a fallen world: "And not only they, but ourselves also, which have the firstfruits of the Spirit, even we ourselves groan within ourselves, waiting for the adoption, to wit, the redemption of our body."

Then, Paul declares through inspiration of the Holy Spirit a precious promise, which has become one of the most quoted promises in the Bible: "And we know that all things work together for good to them that love God, to them who are the called according to his purpose." God takes the difficult, the mind-numbing, the tragic circumstances of our broken, corrupt world and in His Divine omnipotence and sovereignty brings these situations to good. However, if we keep our heads bent low as we trudge along, shielding our faces from the rain and struggling with our burdens, we often miss God's ultimate plan. Even though everything is dragging us down, we must force ourselves to look up, patiently searching for God's goodness to emerge in the troubled circumstance. If we don't give up hope, we may just begin to see a rainbow.

Reflection

What good can you imagine emerging from the difficult or discouraging circumstances you face?

_____

_____

_____

_____

Why can you trust in the goodness of God—that He will bring good from the bad?

_____

_____

_____

_____

How will you cultivate hope in your situation?

_____

_____

_____

_____

 Where the Rubber Meets the Road

God brings good out of the worst situations for those who love Him.

Part Ten

Remembering My Heavenly Destination

But lay up for yourselves treasures in heaven, where neither moth nor rust doth corrupt, and where thieves do not break through nor steal: For where your treasure is, there will your heart be also. Matthew 6:20-21 (KJV)

Day 29

No More Decay

Scripture Reading: Matthew 6:19-24

Promise from God: But lay up for yourselves treasures in heaven, where neither moth nor rust doth corrupt, and where thieves do not break through nor steal: For where your treasure is, there will your heart be also.

Matthew 6:20-21 (KJV)

My heart sank when I saw a small hole in a favorite dress; then I noticed a tear in the sleeve of my husband's suit jacket. Somehow a moth had invaded our closet. I worried about how we would get this pesky creature out of our house. I didn't want my clothing to smell like moth-balls! Fortunately, my husband came up with a natural-based remedy that worked—no more moths.

In Matthew chapter 6, Jesus used moths to illustrate the corruption of our earth and the futility of investing in temporal possessions. He said, "But lay up for yourselves treasures in heaven, where neither moth nor rust doth corrupt, and where thieves do not break through nor steal: For where your treasure is, there will your heart be also" (Matthew 6:20-21). Have you ever contemplated the many hours we spend warding off corruption and trying to preserve temporal things? Our money and energy go into replacing lichen-covered roofs; preventing or patching rust spots on our vehicles; and eradicating insects like termites, ants, and wasps. Day by day, everything in our world ages. Our bodies are similarly waning. We are urged to eat healthy, exercise, go for regular check-ups, and stay mentally and physically fit if we want to live a long life. However, because of sin's curse, our bodies are all destined eventually to die.

The wonderful promise for the Christian is our bodies are only a case or a shell for our real selves. If we spend our lives investing in our own soul and the souls of others, our treasure rests in Heaven.

In our eternal home, we will no longer have to work to maintain possessions or our bodies. Moths, rust, and mold will no longer eat away at our homes and belongings. No more time need be spent on maintaining our corruptible bodies. We will enjoy glorious and perfect bodies. We will struggle no more with cancer, heart disease, and pain; we will no longer have to watch our loved ones suffer. As Paul writes in I Corinthians 15:54, "So when this corruptible shall have put on incorruption, and this mortal shall have put on immortality, then shall be brought to pass the saying that is written, Death is swallowed up in victory."

Earthly problems often remind us of how transient our possessions are and how fragile our physical bodies become over time. Whenever we face a difficulty that threatens to overwhelm our spirits, we must remember nothing will harm our souls if we keep them in God's hands. Jesus said while our possessions and bodies are vulnerable, our true treasure is untouchable by earthly decay. Therefore, we must live every moment for eternity.

Reflection

How are you laying up treasure in Heaven?

_____
_____
_____
_____

Make a list of your top three priorities below. Be honest about this list. If you find your relationship with God slipping to second or third place, ask God to help you to focus first on Him. Lay up eternal treasure.

_____
_____
_____
_____

What will you do today that will have eternal value?

_____
_____
_____
_____

 Where the Rubber Meets the Road

Our eternal, incorruptible treasure rests in Heaven.

Dwelling with God

Day 30

Scripture Reading: Revelation 21:1-7

Promise from God: And I heard a great voice out of heaven saying, Behold, the tabernacle of God *is* with men, and he will dwell with them, and they shall be his people, and God himself shall be with them, *and be* their God. And God shall wipe away all tears from their eyes; and there shall be no more death, neither sorrow, nor crying, neither shall there be any more pain: for the former things are passed away.

Revelation 21:3-4 (KJV)

M any years before I was born, my grandfather was killed in a car accident at the age of 34. He left behind diary entries of the four days preceding his sudden death. In these journal entries, he talks of praying for an hour each morning, of fasting meals, of being guided by the Holy Spirit, of attending worship services, and of making apologies for speaking without thinking. He wants to have "an unbroken fellowship with God," and he records praying "in search of deeper things in [the] Lord." A wistful feeling pervades his writing; he anticipates something wonderful will happen to him soon: "There seems to be a holy fire in the air. I trust [for] a revival or our Lord's coming!" The entry is dated October 13, 1968. A few days later, he was in Heaven. As a young husband, father, and pastor, my grandfather faced many difficulties in his life; but he had learned the secret of living— dwelling with God. Problems in his church, his wife's failing eyesight, the challenges of raising three young children on a small income—all these things did not distract my grandfather from spending time with God. He constantly kept his Heavenly destination in view, and he is dwelling there now—forever in the presence of God.

The problems of this life threaten to overwhelm us at times. However, in Revelation 21:4, the Apostle John declares that in Heaven, God's children will finally be free of persistent pain: "God shall wipe away all tears from their eyes; and there shall be no more death, neither sorrow, nor crying, neither shall there be any more pain: for the former things are passed away." Troubled relationships, abusive family situations, estranged friendships, broken marriages, unhappy homes—these things will not exist in Heaven. Disease, disability, mental illness, pain, and suffering—they will no longer impair us or our loved ones. We will be free at last from grief: no more sorrow, no more tears, no more goodbyes, and no more darkness or night.

Beyond all this, Heaven will be Heaven because God is there. Revelation 21:3 is perhaps the culminating promise of the Bible. The Apostle John says: "And I heard a great voice out of heaven saying, Behold, the tabernacle of God *is* with men, and he will dwell with them, and they shall be his people, and God himself shall be with them, *and be* their God." As His children, we will dwell continually with God—always to feel His unmistakable presence, always to bask in the warmth of His Spirit. He shall be with us forever. We will see Him; we will touch Him. Eternal communion with God—it is beyond our comprehension.

However, we will not dwell with God throughout eternity if we do not dwell with Him on this earth. God must be our God on earth if He will be our God in eternity. My grandfather's journal account remains a faithful reminder to me of how to implement heavenly priorities in the dirt and grime of daily living. Prayer, fasting, praise, worship, restitution—these disciplines keep our celestial destination in view. Spending time with God each day makes the promise of Revelation 21:3 grow more precious: "Behold, the tabernacle of God *is* with men, and he will dwell with them, and they shall be his people, and God himself shall be with them, *and be* their God."

Reflection

Spend a few minutes writing about your mental image of Heaven based on Scripture.

_____

_____

_____

_____

How do Scriptures about Heaven give you comfort?

_____

_____

_____

_____

Finish this thought: Thank You, Father, for preparing a heavenly home for me. I praise You that _____

_____

_____ .

 Where the Rubber Meets the Road

We will spend eternity with God in Heaven if we spend our time on earth with Him.

Even So Come, Lord Jesus

Scripture Reading: I Thessalonians 4:13-18

Promise from God: For the Lord himself shall descend from heaven with a shout, with the voice of the archangel, and with the trump of God: and the dead in Christ shall rise first: Then we which are alive and remain shall be caught up together with them in the clouds, to meet the Lord in the air: and so shall we ever be with the Lord.

I Thessalonians 4:16-17 (KJV)

It is drizzling rain, and I am standing in the night, lit only by our van's headlights. It has not been an ordinary day. I have buried my baby boy. He is not at home snug in his crib—cooing, crying, and expanding his lusty lungs. He is dead. This morning, family and friends joined my husband and me around the little white box, adorned with a huge mound of white lilies. Aaron's committal service was a beautiful moment of soaring song, Scripture, and balloons.

But now it is dark, and I find myself back at the graveside. I am compelled to go there on this rainy, moonless night to make sure my baby is properly buried, to see with my own eyes the little box is protected from the wind and the predators that roam at night. As Aaron's Mama, I should be swaddling his little body safely at home, but I am not. Instead, I am here in this dark, clammy graveyard, making sure my son is properly "tucked in" for the long night. And as I stand over the grave, I remember the words of I Thessalonians chapter four, my baby boy is "asleep" in Christ.

Even though I can't see the surrounding gravestones in the dark, I think of the others resting here: Michael's grandfather and other elderly saints from our family church. Some I have known; others are strangers. I think also of the babies and toddlers buried around my son. Carson, Anthony, Timothy, and Wesley, all taken as babies and toddlers, sons of our friends or family, leaving their mothers' arms empty.

As I kneel down, my face pressed near the white lilies atop my son's grave, a beautiful picture suddenly bursts on my mental sight. I envision the Second Return of Christ. For one brief second, I imagine the little children and the elderly saints sleeping in the graveyard around me, suddenly rousing to the sound of the trumpet and rising together.

I stand up and walk back to the van and my family, returning to the ebb and flow of my life, comforted by the Scripture: "But I would not have you to be ignorant, brethren, concerning them which are asleep, that ye sorrow not even as others which have no hope. For if we believe that Jesus died and rose again, even so them also which sleep in Jesus will God bring with him" (I Thessalonians 4: 13-14).

A month passes. It is morning, daybreak. I am walking to the graveyard, carrying a small wreath of flowers. It is not the first time I have visited my baby's grave since that cold, rainy night, the day we buried him. I was here on Mother's Day with my husband and oldest son to place a teddy bear on the grass mound. I have visited on my daily walks, pushing my toddler son in his stroller—the butterflies dancing in the meadows and the birds singing in the trees. Countless ordinary afternoons, I have come here. As spring graduation ceremonies are conducted at the school just down the road, I have sat here and cried. My son will never graduate from kindergarten, high school, or college. The tears fall as I think of all the hopes and dreams for my son's life that died with him.

And now, I stand over the grave at sunrise. I stuff into a garbage bag the dead funeral flowers, the bouquet of shriveled white lilies, and I bend down and place a little wreath of blue silk flowers on the grave. The sun now rising embraces me with warmth. I think of how my son's grave faces the East, and the line of an old hymn plays in my mind, "Some golden daybreak, Jesus will come." Again, I see the sleeping children and adults rising to meet their God, their Creator, their Savior.

The words of the hymn keep going through my mind as I walk back to my home in the sunrise, "Some golden daybreak, Jesus will come." And I think, surely this must be the greatest promise of all: "Then we

Puddles and Rubber Boots

which are alive and remain shall be caught up together with them in the clouds, to meet the Lord in the air: and so shall we ever be with the Lord."

Reflection

In your own words, explain the first and second resurrections. Read about the first resurrection in Matthew 28, Mark 16, Luke 24, and John 20. Then, reread I Thessalonians 4:13-18.

_____

_____

_____

_____

How can you avoid sorrowing as they "which have no hope"?

_____

_____

_____

_____

How does your faith and hope rest in the death and resurrection of Jesus Christ?

_____

_____

_____

_____

 Where the Rubber Meets the Road

Some golden daybreak, Jesus will come. Even so come, Lord Jesus.

Afterward

While I was finishing this devotional book, our basement flooded. We had a thunderstorm with torrential rain, which rushed off the mountain and replenished the underground springs. The water was running through our basement cinderblock walls like several bathroom faucets on full blast. My husband was up all night and the next day, pumping out about a foot of water every few hours from our basement.

And I found myself donning rubber boots, clomping down the stairs, and splashing through the ice cold, mountain water. I tried to gather our belongings, which were floating and bobbing on the swimming pool forming underneath our home. Fortunately, most of the stuff stored in the basement we planned on putting in a yard sale or sending to the thrift store.

"I guess you don't want us to have a yard sale," I joked with God as we carried the damaged stuff up to the truck to haul to the dumpster. A few of my childhood mementos, like diaries and books, were damaged, and I was surprised to find it did not bother me. It was just stuff; eventually one day I would have to let go. Apparently, God wanted me to let go now.

I felt peace and calm assurance in the flooded basement. God's promises were still carrying me. Even though the storm had flooded my earthly home, I realized nothing could touch my Divine refuge—my faith in God's Word or His Nature.

"I know you have a purpose in all this," I prayed. "Thank you, God, for being with me in the storm. I'm waiting expectantly to see what good you will bring from it."

Dear reader, I pray the meditations in this book have been an encouragement to you. I hope our Mighty God has strengthened your faith as you have read the Scriptures and God's sweet promises. I encourage you: keep reading the Bible with me, and let's keep joining in prayer. Though we may never meet on this earth, some day we will be together in eternity. Though I may not know your name, I am praying for you. You can weather the storm through God's infinite grace.

Acknowledgements

I want to thank my husband, who has always encouraged and supported me through all my endeavors. Thank you for loving me and caring for me. I also thank you for the time you spent on this project: reading my manuscript, working on the photography, and offering me lots of advice and encouragement.

I want to thank my mom, Barbara, for her unconditional love; my dad, Richard, for always believing in me; my sister, Joanna, for all her endless help; my brother, William, and his wife, Nicole, for their faithful love.

My mom and sister spent considerable time listening to me and reading and commenting on my devotional. Thanks for believing in me and supporting me. Thank you, Mom and Dad, for the financial investment in my writing ministry.

I also want to acknowledge my husband's family. I hope this book is an encouragement to you in your own storms.

In writing this book, I have had time to pause and reflect over my life's journey and the many people who have walked with me during storms in my life. They have splashed right through many mud puddles with me, encouraging and believing in me. Many of these women have triumphed over their own difficult storms and serve as my "great cloud of witnesses," a source of constant inspiration. Thank you to a host of family, friends, and mentors whose influence has forever touched my life.

Thank you to the wonderful authors and editors who gave me encouragement when I needed it.

To my critique group companions, Judith DeStefano and Erika Gingrich, thanks for listening and for your honest advice. I also want to thank Frances Stetler for critiquing my manuscript and Crystal Gingrigh for proofreading it. Any mistakes remaining in the book are entirely my own.

Most of all I want to thank God for loving, redeeming, sanctifying, and keeping me. Without Him there would be no book.

About the Author

I am a wife and mother. My primary vocation is assisting my husband in full-time ministry and raising my young son. I enjoy my life! Pursuing God's will and the Great Commission are great passions of mine.

Professionally, I have undergraduate degrees in English and education. I served as a teacher for seven years and a pastor's wife for two years. My husband and I conduct child evangelism ministry, and my husband is a Christian school educator.

I blog at http://www.jeaniefritz.com/. Consider visiting my site and joining my email list to learn about my upcoming books and to receive a monthly newsletter of encouragement. I would also love to connect with you on Facebook, Twitter, Instagram, Pinterest, Good Reads, Amazon, and YouTube.

I hope this little book has touched your life and drawn you closer to God.

Love,
Jeanie Fritz

50617780R00067

Made in the USA
Columbia, SC
09 February 2019